# MONSTER MADNESS

## RIDDLES · JOKES · FUN

# by Joseph Rosenbloom
## Illustrations by Joyce Behr

**WINGS BOOKS**
**New York**

To Danielle Backerman with love

This 1991 edition is published by Wings Books,
distributed by Outlet Book Company, Inc., a Random House Company,
225 Park Avenue South, New York, New York 10003, by arrangement
with Sterling Publishing Co., Inc.

Printed and bound in the United States of America

Library of Congress Cataloging-in-Publication Data
Rosenbloom, Joseph.
    Monster madness : riddles, jokes, fun / by Joseph Rosenbloom :
illustrations by Joyce Behr.
        p.   cm.
    Summary: A collection of riddles, jokes, and tongue twisters about
monsters.
    ISBN 0-517-07354-4
    1. Monsters—Juvenile humor.    2. Wit and humor, Juvenile.
3. Riddles, Juvenile.    [1. Monsters—Wit and humor.    2. Riddles.
3. Jokes.]    I. Behr, Joyce, ill.    II. Title.
[PN6231.M665R6 1991]
818'.5402—dc20                                        91-28087
                                                       CIP
                                                        AC

ISBN 0-517-07354-4
8   7   6   5   4   3   2   1

# Contents

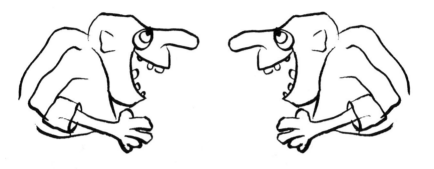

# 1 Warm Ups

What kind of mistakes do ghosts make?
*Boo-boos.*

How can you tell a skeleton from an elephant?
*It's hard to get into a revolving door with an elephant.*

How do you keep a monster from smelling?
*Cut off his nose.*

Did you hear what happened to the ghoul who fell down the well?
*He kicked the bucket.*

What is worse than being bitten by Count Dracula?
*Shaking hands with Captain Hook.*

What kind of ant is ten feet tall?
*A gi-ant.*

What do you get when a giant walks through a potato field?
*Mashed potatoes.*

What beans do cannibals like?
*Human beans.*

BYSTANDER: Have an accident?
VICTIM: No, thanks. I just had one.

Where was Count Dracula when the lights went out?
*In the dark.*

When is Count Dracula like a beggar?
*When he puts the bite on you.*

When is Count Dracula not a vampire?
*When he turns into a street.*

What did the witch say to her small broom?
*"Go to sweep, wittle baby."*

What would you get if you crossed a witch and a millionaire?
*You would get a witch (rich) person.*

What would you get if you crossed a shark with a parrot?
*An animal that could talk your ear off.*

What would you get if you crossed a snake and a funeral?
*You'd get a hiss and a hearse.*

What is small, lives underground, and solves crimes?
*Sherlock Gnomes (Holmes).*

Why did the museum show an old mummy?
*Because it couldn't afford a new one.*

SPIRIT: May I haunt your castle?
KING: Certainly—be my ghost!

What is a demon's favorite dessert?
  *Devil's food cake.*

FLIP: Is it true that a monster won't hurt you if you
  carry a flashlight?
FLOP: That depends on how fast you carry it.

Why is the Invisible Man a poor liar?
  *Because anyone can see right through him.*

What is Count Dracula's favorite candy?
*An all-day sucker.*

How can you tell King Kong from a banana?
*The banana is yellow.*

Why is the letter G scary?
*Because it turns a host into a ghost.*

What did the skeleton say when it got a comb for its birthday?
*"I'll never part with it."*

What is a zombie's favorite stone?
*A tombstone.*

How do zombies speak?
*In a grave voice.*

What do sea monsters eat?
*Fish and ships.*

Why did Dr. Jekyll go to Florida?
*To tan his Hyde (hide).*

Who is Count Dracula's favorite composer?
*Ludwing von Bat-hoven (Ludwig van Beethoven).*

What happened to Ludwig van Beethoven after he died?
*He decomposed.*

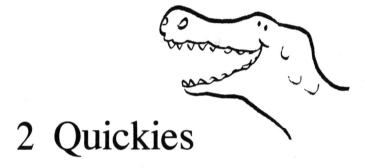

# 2 Quickies

What color is a ghost?
*Boo (blue)!*

What is a ghost's favorite thing on a farm?
*The scarecrow.*

FIRST GHOST: My girlfriend is a medium.
SECOND GHOST: Is that so? Mine is a large.

What happens when a banana sees a ghost?
*The banana splits.*

What is the expression on a zombie's face?
*Deadpan.*

Do zombies enjoy being dead?
*Of corpse! Of corpse!*

NURSE: Doctor, there's an invisible man in your waiting room.
DOCTOR: Tell him I can't see him.

How do you disguise a mummy?
*With masking tape.*

What is a mummy after it's 2,000 years old?
*2,001 years old.*

What comes out at night and goes "Flap! Flap! Chomp! Ouch!"
*A vampire with a sore tooth.*

How do you say vampire in Spanish?
*"Vampire in Spanish."*

Why does Count Dracula wear a black belt?
*To keep his pants up.*

Where does dragon (draggin') milk come from?
*From short cows.*

Where does an Indian ghost sleep?
*In a creepy teepee.*

What does the hangman read every morning?
*The noosepaper (newspaper).*

Why did the female ghoul go on a diet?
*To keep her ghoulish (girlish) figure.*

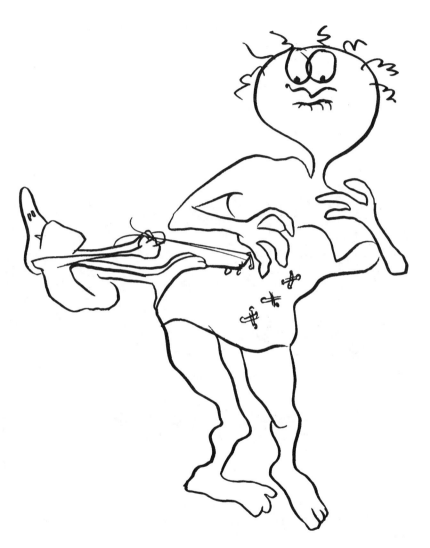

What snack do werewolves enjoy?
*Ladyfingers.*

What do ghouls eat for breakfast?
*Shrouded (Shredded) Wheat.*

What do ghosts eat in an Italian restaurant?
*Spook-ghetti (spaghetti).*

What kind of keys open a tomb?
*Skeleton keys.*

What do you call a skeleton that doesn't like to work?
*Lazybones.*

What do you get if you cross a skeleton with a jar of peanut butter?

*Bones in your peanut butter sandwiches.*

What do you get if you cross a peanut butter sandwich and a werewolf?

*A sandwich that gets hairy and howls when the moon is full.*

What ghost haunts a clock?

*The spirit of the times.*

How does a witch tell time?

*With a witch watch.*

What is purple and eats people?

*A purple people eater.*

"And how much would you like to contribute to the Indian relief fund, Mrs. Custer?"

Why do dinosaurs lie down?

*Because they can't lie up.*

Why do witches fly on broomsticks?

*It beats walking.*

Why do ghosts like to take elevators?

*It raises their spirits.*

What kind of raincoat does a ghoul wear on a rainy day?

*A wet one.*

# SAY THESE 3 TIMES QUICKLY

(HA-HA!)

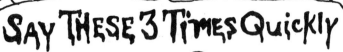

The Abominable Snowman seeks six thick sticks.

Mummies munch much mush;
Monsters munch much mush;
Many mummies and monsters
Must munch much mush.

Should a shark share swordfish steak?

# 3 Freaky Firsts

What do monsters drink during warm weather?
*Ice-ghoul (cool) lemonade.*

What do you do with a green monster?
*Wait until he ripens.*

BOY MONSTER: Did you ever see anyone like me before?
GIRL MONSTER: Yes, once. But I had to pay admission.

What part of you moves when you dream about a ghoul?

*Your flesh crawls.*

When do vampires annoy you most?

*When they get under your skin.*

How do people feel after they have been bitten by a vampire?

*Holier.*

What newspaper did the dinosaurs read?

*The Prehistoric Times.*

What do you call an invisible man who pilots a space ship?
*An astro-naught (astronaut).*

What do you get if you cross a chicken with a ghost?
*A peck-a-boo.*

What is a ghost's favorite show?
*My Fear (Fair) Lady.*

At what age do ghosts make the most noise?
*When they're groan (grown) up.*

What happened when the boy ghost met the girl ghost?
*It was love at first fright.*

What's better than presence of mind when you meet a vampire?
*Absence of body.*

What kind of a dog does Count Dracula own?
*A bloodhound.*

Who is Count Dracula's favorite crime fighter?
*Batman.*

What did Count Dracula say when he bit Santa Claus?
*"This is going to sleigh you!"*

What is the first thing you put in a graveyard?
*Your feet.*

What is a ghoul's favorite food?
*Goulash.*

What is a ghoul's favorite vegetable juice?
*Tomb-ato (tomato) juice.*

How can you tell if there's a giant in your sandwich?
*It's hard to lift.*

How do you make a monster stew?
*Keep it waiting for two hours.*

What statesman led France for many years?
*Charles de Ghoul (Gaulle).*

Why did the mummy become famous when it caught fire?
*It was the last of the red hot mummies.*

What kind of career did the zombie choose?
*It became a professional dyer (die-er).*

What kind of tale does a little vampire like to hear at bedtime?
*A gory story.*

What time is it when Count Dracula leaves his coffin?
*Time to run.*

# 4 Monster Math

A zombie walked into a store and ordered a small coke. He put down a ten dollar bill to pay for it. The clerk thought that zombies knew nothing about money, and so he handed the zombie 50 cents in change.

The clerk watched as the zombie sipped his coke. Finally, curiosity got the best of him.

"I didn't know zombies enjoyed cokes," he said. "We don't get too many zombies in the store."

"No wonder," the zombie replied, "at nine dollars and fifty cents a coke."

# SAY THESE 3 TIMES QUICKLY

(HO-HO!)

The glum ghoul grows glummer.

The haunted cheap chip shop sells cheap chips to haunted ships.

Frankenstein favors five free fruit floats.

Flo fled Bigfoot Friday.

"Six small slick seals," said the skeleton.

The witch bewitched the thin twin tinsmith.

Which witch bewitched which watch?

What would you get if you crossed a monster and a chicken?

*I don't know what you'd call it, but it would always be in a fowl (foul) mood.*

Why couldn't Count Dracula write any more checks?

*Because he was overdrawn at the blood bank.*

What time is it when Count Dracula goes to the dentist?

*Tooth-hurty (2:30).*

What happens when Count Dracula gets angry?

*He sees red.*

What has four "I's" (eyes) and sleeps in a water bed?

*The Mississippi.*

What has twenty heads but can't think?

*A book of matches.*

What do you get if you cross a goat and a monster?

*An animal that eats a path to your door.*

What do you get if you cross a monster and an owl?

*An animal that frightens people but doesn't give a hoot.*

What do you get if you cross a monster and a rabbit?

*I don't know what you'd call it, but you'd have hundreds in a month.*

What kind of tests do they give in witch school?

*Hex-aminations (examinations).*

Who belongs to the monster's PTA?

*Mummies and deadies.*

"He lost both legs in a train wreck last year."
"Did the railroad treat him right?"
"He can't kick."

Sign in funeral home:
SATISFACTION GUARANTEED OR DOUBLE YOUR MUMMY BACK

If in going into an enchanted forest you saw 20 monsters on your right, and 20 monsters on your left when returning home, how many monsters would you count?

*Twenty. You counted the same monsters going and coming.*

How many ghouls can fit into an empty casket?

*One. After that the casket isn't empty anymore.*

"You and your suicide attempts. Just look at this gas bill!"

When do you charge a Frankenstein monster?

*When he can't pay cash.*

PING: Did you hear about the new chocolate bar called Jaws?
PONG: No—what does it cost?
PING: An arm and a leg.

Why did the monster chase its tail?

*It was trying to make both ends meet.*

"Daddy, why can't I play with the other kids?"
"Shut up and deal!"

How does a monster count to 33?

*On his fingers.*

When are dinosaurs easiest to catch?

*When their scales give them away (a weigh).*

How do you cut a dinosaur in two?
   *With a dino-saw.*

# 5 Monster Manners

What should you watch when you're talking to an angry monster?

*Your step.*

BOY MONSTER: Give me a kiss before supper.
GIRL MONSTER: What? And spoil my appetite?

What do you eat for supper when a haunted house burns down?

*Roast ghost.*

How do ghosts eat food?

*By gobblin' it.*

Did you hear about the monster girl who had a coming out party?

*They made her go back in again.*

Which dragon eats with its tail?

*They all do. No dragon removes its tail to eat.*

Is it all right to eat pickles with your fingers?

*No, eat the pickles first—then eat your fingers.*

Why was the gravedigger so well liked?

*Because he was such a down-to-earth guy.*

What did the big ghost say to the little ghost when they entered the car?

*"Fasten your sheet (seat) belt."*

Why doesn't a giant's nose measure more than 11 inches?

> *If it measured more than 11 inches, it would be a foot.*

How do witches on broomsticks drink their tea?
> *Out of flying saucers.*

What is a ghost's favorite day?
> *Moanday.*

What does a ghost bride throw to her bridesmaids?
> *Her boo-quet (bouquet).*

What do you call a person who sticks his right arm down a shark's throat?
> *Lefty.*

What did the mother ghost say to the baby ghost?
*"It isn't polite to spook until you are spooken to."*

What steps do you take when you're chased by a giant?
*Giant steps.*

Do giants ever help people get smaller?
*Yes, people often shrink from them.*

What did the police do when the giant took the road to town?
*They made him put it back.*

What is the best way to talk to a vampire?
*By long distance.*

Why do people avoid Count Dracula?
*Because he's a pain in the neck.*

GUDENOV: Why do people take advantage of Count Dracula?
BADENOV: Because people never give a sucker an even break.

Why does King Kong watch everything he says and does?
*Because he doesn't want to make a monkey of himself.*

What do you say to King Kong when he gets married?
*Kong-gratulations (congratulations).*

What did Count Dracula say after he stopped biting the girl's neck?
*"It's been nice gnawing you."*

"Did you fall down that elevator shaft?"
"No, I was sitting here and they built it around me."

How do you treat a sick monster?
*With respect.*

What do you do with a blue monster?
*Cheer him up.*

OSCAR: "When I die, I want to be cremated."
FELIX: "That would be just like you, to go away and leave ashes all over the house."

Which flowers decorate a zombie's tomb?
*Mari-ghouls and mourning-gories (marigolds and morning-glories).*

Who greets people at the door of a haunted house?
*The ghost host.*

What happened to the zombie who swallowed a spoon?
*He couldn't stir.*

What do you call it when a bunch of mummies get together to talk things over?
*A wrap (rap) session.*

What do you call a clean, nice, hardworking, friendly monster?

*A failure.*

What did the boy monster say to the girl monster?

*"You sure have a nice pair of legs, nice pair of legs, nice pair of legs."*

What do you call a monster who eats his mother and father?

*An orphan.*

What do you say when you meet a two-headed monster?

*"Hello, hello!"*

# SAY THESE 3 TIMES QUICKLY

### (HEE-HEE!)

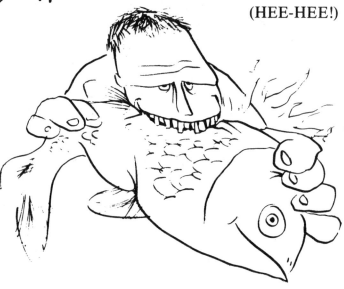

Frankenstein feasted on flaming fish at the free fish fry.

Frankenstein flies through fog and frost to fight flu fast.

Frankenstein threw three free throws.

The flimsy phantom fled the flood-filled flat.

Faint phantoms fear fat flat flounders.

What do you call a 2,000-pound giant with a short temper?

*"Sir!"*

What do you do when a giant sneezes?

*Get out of the way.*

What do you get if you cross a giant and a computer?

*The biggest know-it-all you ever saw.*

# 6 Seeking Mr. Hyde

How do you get in touch with a shark?
*Drop him a line.*

Where does Dr. Jekyll go to get some privacy?
*To his Hyde-a-way (hideaway).*

Where does Mr. Hyde go to get some privacy?
*To Jekylloslovakia (Czechoslovakia).*

Where do ghouls go to get an education?
*To ghoul school.*

Who protects the shores where ghosts live?
*The Ghost (Coast) Guard.*

Who is the main ghost in the United States Congress?
*The Spooker (Speaker) of the House.*

Where does a witch keep her wallet?
*In a hag bag.*

FLIP: Did you hear the joke about the witch's broom?
FLOP: No, I haven't.
FLIP: That's strange. It's sweeping the nation.

FIRST WITCH: I had to drop out of charm school.
SECOND WITCH: What happened?
FIRST WITCH: I flunked spelling.

If two mummies ring your bell, what do you have?
*Dead ringers.*

If the stork brings human babies, who brings the giant babies?
*Cranes.*

Why did the giant jog every morning?
*To get his extra-size (exercise).*

Did you hear about the monster who had such a repulsive personality that when he threw a boomerang it wouldn't come back?

What American does Count Dracula admire most?
*A full-blooded Indian.*

Where do ghosts buy their sheets?
*In a boo-tique.*

Why are vampire families so close?
*Because blood is thicker than water.*

Why did the girl break up with the giant?
*She was afraid he might have a crush on her.*

What did the giant say when he sat on the box of Girl Scout cookies?
*"That's how the cookie crumbles."*

Why was the giant arrested when he set out on a trip?
*Because he hit the road.*

Why wasn't the Invisible Man popular at parties?
*He wasn't much to look at.*

What animal does Count Dracula admire most?
*A giraffe.*

What is Count Dracula's favorite fruit?
*A neck-tarine (nectarine).*

When is a werewolf most likely to enter a house?
*When the door is open.*

Why did the ghost child measure himself against the wall?
*He wanted to know if he gruesome (grew some).*

What keeps a monster from being a good dancer?
*His three left feet.*

Who won the monster beauty contest?
*No one.*

NIT: What is the difference between a monster and
a matterbaby?
WIT: What's a "matterbaby"?
NIT: Nothing, sweetie. What's the matter with you?

How did King Kong escape from his cage?
*He used a monkey wrench.*

How do you stop an angry monster from charging?
*Take away his credit cards.*

Why is a haunted house like a rabbit farm?
*They are both hair (hare) raising places.*

What do you get when a ghost haunts a dairy farm?
*Milk shakes.*

# 7 Games Monsters Play

What game do ghost children like to play?
*Haunt-and-seek.*

What did the ocean say to the shark?
*It didn't say anything—it just waved.*

What part of a book is like a shark?
*The fin-ish.*

When is a giant not a giant?
*When he catches cold he becomes a little horse (hoarse).*

What is a monster's favorite necklace?
*A choker.*

What game do monster children play?
*Hyde-and-sick.*

What two things can't a monster ever have for breakfast?
*Lunch and dinner.*

Knock, knock.
    Who's there?
King Kong.
    King Kong who?
"King Kong (ding, dong) the witch is dead . . ."

Why did the monster mother knit her son three socks?

*Because he grew another foot.*

How can you tell when witches are carrying a time bomb?

*You can hear their brooms tick.*

LITTLE BOY: Daddy, when were you in Egypt?
FATHER: Egypt? I never was in Egypt.
LITTLE BOY: Then where did you get my mummy?

What is green and wrinkled and goes through walls?

*Casper, the friendly pickle.*

What do ghosts like to ride at the amusement park?
*The roller ghoster (coaster).*

What game do ghost children like to play?
*Peek-a-boo!*

What is a ghost's favorite dessert?
*High scream (ice cream).*

What do ghosts chew?
*Boo-ble (bubble) gum.*

What kind of music do ghosts write?
*Sheet music.*

Did Dr. Frankenstein amuse his monster?
*Yes, he kept him in stitches.*

GIRL GHOUL: Do you love me?
BOY GHOUL: Madly! I would die for you.
GIRL GHOUL: You always say that, but you never do it!

Why did the ghost haunt the lamp?
*Because it was a light sleeper.*

How do you make a banana split?
*Yell, "Boo!"*

If you were walking along a dark street and met a Frankenstein monster, a ghost, a werewolf, and a mummy, what should you hope for?
*Hope it's Halloween.*

If a werewolf lost his tail, where could he get another?

*At a retail store.*

Why are skeletons like blank applications?
*Because their forms have not been filled out.*

What do you call a skeleton who's a good friend?
*A bony crony.*

What do monsters have that no one else has?
*Baby monsters.*

What did the mother ghost say when her ghost child went out to play?
*"Be careful you don't get your sheets dirty!"*

What do witches ring for in a hotel?
*B-room service.*

Why did the monster go out with the prune?
*Because he couldn't get a date.*

Why can't the Invisible Man ever be a true friend?
*Because he can only be a nodding (nothing) acquaintance.*

Who writes cookbooks for vampires?
*Batty (Betty) Crocker.*

How can you tell if a vampire has been in your tomato juice?
*By the two tiny teeth marks on the lid.*

What ghost helps win games?
*The team spirit.*

What do you call a group of zombie dancers?
  *A corpse (corps) de ballet.*

# 8 Creature Features

How do you make a strawberry shake?
*Take it to a horror movie.*

What do you say about a terrible mummy movie?
*"It sphinx!"*

What do you call a great scary film?
*A terror-ific movie.*

What is dangerous, yellow and hot?
*Shark-infested custard.*

What would happen if a giant sat in front of you at the movies?

*You'd miss most of the film.*

Why is it good to tell ghost stories in hot weather?
*Because they are so chilling.*

FIRST UNDERTAKER: Poor Sam! He died from drinking shellac.

SECOND UNDERTAKER: Well, at least he had a fine finish.

When the executioner registered at the hotel, the clerk asked him what kind of room he desired. The executioner explained, "My needs are small. I just want a place to hang my hat and a few friends."

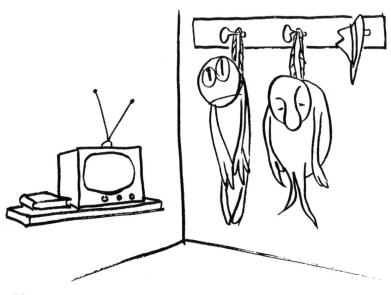

Why was the werewolf hired by the radio station?
*Because he had the paws (pause) for station identification.*

Where do ghouls like to sit when they go to the theatre?
*In dead center.*

What happens to the actors when a ghost haunts a theater?
*They get stage fright.*

What haunting melody do ghouls sing early in the day?

"*Oh, what a beautiful mourning (morning) . . .*"

What kind of eyes does Count Dracula admire?
*Bloodshot.*

"Mommy, quick, where are the marshmallows? Marvin's on fire!"

What's the best way to raise King Kong?
*With a jack.*

Where do supernatural creatures live?
*In a ghost town.*

How did they ship skeletons in the Old West?
*By Bony (Pony) Express.*

What happened to Jesse James after a vampire bit him?
*He was a sick shooter.*

"Mom, the steam roller just ran over brother!"
"Well, I can't come out now—just slip him under the door."

How does a dinosaur get to Carnegie Hall?
*By practicing his scales.*

# SAY THESE 3 TIMES QUICKLY

### (HEY-HEY!)

The wretched witch watched a walrus washing. Did the wretched witch watch a walrus washing? If the wretched witch watched a walrus washing, where's the washing walrus the wretched witch watched?

The ghost goes by Blue Goose bus.

Monsters chomp cheap cherry marshmallows.

The shark shops for short silk shorts.

The shark slashes sheets.

Why wasn't the ghost successful?
*Because it didn't believe in itself.*

What do you get when you cross a werewolf with Lassie?
*A pedigreed monster.*

What do you get when you cross a werewolf with a boat?
*A wolf in ship's clothing.*

What do you get when you cross a werewolf with a vampire?
*A fur coat that sticks close to your neck.*

Who sits at the desk in front of the class in monster school?

*The creature teacher.*

IGOR: What is the plot of that new science fiction movie?

BORIS: It's the same old story: boy meets girl, boy loses girl, boy builds new girl.

TV ANNOUNCER: "Because of the following special program, the Invisible Man will not be seen tonight."

What resembles a blob and has chrome stripes?

*A deluxe blob.*

NIT: Did you hear about the monster rip-off?

WIT: No. What did they rip off?

NIT: Arms, legs, heads . . ."

How far can you walk into a cemetery?

*Only halfway. After that you're walking out.*

What is the difference between a monster and a loaf of bread?

*Well, if you don't know, remind me not to send you out for any groceries.*

What do ghosts eat for breakfast?

*Scream of Wheat.*

What kind of shots do ghost children take to prevent disease?

*Boo-ster shots.*

It is a lovely summer evening and Johnny and Sue are parked on a hill overlooking town. Johnny turns to Sue and says, "Sue, sweetheart, I have some good news and some bad news. The good news is that at any moment we can see a lovely full moon rise over the hill."

Oh, you're so romantic," Sue says. "What is the bad news?"

"I'm a werewolf! Aaargh!"

What happened to the wolf who fell into the washing machine?

*He became a wash-and-werewolf.*

"Mom, what is a werewolf?"

*"Shut up, kid, and comb your face!"*

FIRST CANNIBAL: I hate my sister-in-law.
SECOND CANNIBAL: Okay. I'll just pass the vegetables.

# 9 Weird Characters

Where should a 300-pound goblin go?
*On a diet.*

How does the Invisible Man look?
*Like nothing you ever saw.*

Two giants are standing on a bridge. One is the father of the other's son. What relation are the two giants?
*Husband and wife.*

What would you get if you crossed a monster and a cat?

*A neighborhood without dogs.*

What would you get if you crossed a monster with a Boy Scout?

*A monster that's always prepared.*

What would you get if you crossed a monster and a parrot?

*I don't know what you'd call it, but if it asks for a cracker, you'd better give it one.*

Why is a zombie a poor liar?
*Because it's a dead giveaway.*

What room does a zombie stay out of?
*The living room.*

Are there any blonde zombies?
*Well, they're not born blonde, but they dye (die) that way.*

What kind of story does a gravedigger like?
*One with a cemetery plot.*

Who writes books about haunted houses?
*Ghost writers.*

How do werewolves study?
*They paw (pore) over their books.*

"Mother made me stop kicking the doctor. I had my new shoes on."

Why are skeletons always calm?
*Because nothing ever gets in their hair.*

What skeleton was a master detective?
*Sherlock Bones (Holmes).*

What is King Kong's favorite flower?
*Chimp-pansies.*

What is grey and prevents forest fires?
*Smokey the Shark.*

In what way is a monster good looking?
*Away off.*

Which side of a werewolf has the most hair?
*The outside.*

What is the difference between a werewolf and a flea?
*A werewolf can have fleas, but a flea can't have werewolves.*

Why are dragons not to be believed?
*Because they are full of hot air.*

# SAY THESE 3 TIMES QUICKLY

## (YUK-YUK!)

The monster muddled the middle melody.

Selfish sharks sell shut shellfish.

Which wristwatch is a Swiss witch's wristwatch?

Which witch wished the wicked wish?

How does a deaf shark hear?
*With a herring (hearing) aid.*

How can you tell a shark from spaghetti?
*The shark doesn't slip off the end of your fork.*

Why do monsters forget so easily?
*Because everything goes in one ear and out the others.*

If you saw nine monsters walking down the street with red socks and one monster walking down the street with green socks, what would this prove?
*That nine out of ten monsters wear red socks.*

What kind of date do ghouls go out with?
*Anybody they can dig up.*

What did the little Pharaoh say to the bully?
*"You leave me alone or I'll tell my mummy!"*

Why did the mummy blush?
*It was wrapped in transparent tape.*

How do you make *one* ghost disappear?
*Add a "g" and you have a* **gone** *ghost.*

How do ghosts keep their hair in place?
*With scare (hair) spray.*

Do people who see ghosts lose their sense of humor?
*Yes, they're scared out of their wits.*

Why does Count Dracula help young vampires?
*Because he likes to see young blood in the business.*

What sound do two vampires make when they kiss?
*"Ouch!"*

Why do witches fly brooms?
*Because vacuum cleaners don't have long enough cords.*

What kind of jewelry do witches wear on their wrists?
*Charm bracelets.*

What piece of jewelry frightens off a vampire?
*A ring around the collar.*

# 10 Aagh!

What doctor do you go to to cure a sick Egyptian mummy?

*A Cairo-practor (chiropractor).*

Why are mummies so nervous?

*Because they are all wound up.*

What do you get when a giant walks through your vegetable garden?

*Squash.*

Why is an evil witch like a candle?
*They are both wick-ed.*

LITTLE DRACULA: Mom, what is a vampire?
MOTHER DRACULA: Shut up, kid, and drink your soup before it clots.

What time is it when a clock strikes 13?
*It's midnight, Pacific Ghost (Coast) Time.*

What did the ghost have for lunch?
*A boo-loney (boloney) sandwich.*

What awful creature can be found in many lunch boxes?
*Sand-wiches (witches).*

How do you run over a dinosaur?
*Climb up its neck, dash along its back, and slide down its tail.*

What do you call monsters' cattle?
*Monsteers.*

What does a monster do before he gets out of his car?
*He kills the engine.*

Why do skeletons catch cold faster than other creatures?
*They get chilled to the bone.*

Where do monsters go when they're sick?
*To a witch doctor.*

What do witches enjoy for a snack on Halloween?
*Hollowwienies.*

JUDGE: Why did you shoot your husband with a bow and arrow?

WOMAN PRISONER: Because I didn't want to wake the children.

How does Count Dracula travel?
*By blood vessel.*

How can you make two vampires out of one?
*Tell it a monster joke and it will double up with laughter.*

Sign in front of a cemetery:
DUE TO A STRIKE, GRAVEDIGGING WILL BE DONE BY A SKELETON CREW

Who brings baby Frankenstein monsters?
*Frankenstorks.*

# SAY THESE 3 Times Quickly

(YECH!)

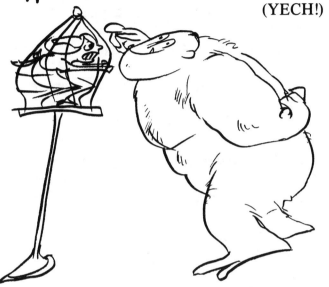

King Kong coops up the cute cook.

The Abominable Snowman slays thirty-three sly, shy thrushes.

How many blocks could a blue Blob break if a blue Blob could break blocks?

The skeleton shops at chop suey shops.

Sixty-six sticky skeletons.

What is the difference between a vampire with a toothache and a rainy day?

*One is roaring with pain, the other is pouring with rain.*

What do you get if you cross a pile of hay with a vampire?

*You get a bale o' Lugosi (Bela Lugosi).*

What do you get if you cross a vampire and a magician?

*A flying sorcerer.*

GHOUL: (*To pharmacist*) I'd like some rat poison.

PHARMACIST: Certainly. Shall I wrap it, or would you like to drink it here?

Knock, knock.

Who's there?

Egypt.

Egypt who?

Egypt me, and I want my mummy back.

When vampires go to jail, where are they kept?

*In blood cells.*

"I guess I've lost another pupil," sighed the professor as his glass eye slid down the drain.

What would you get if you crossed a dog and a vampire?

*I don't know what you'd call it, but its bite would be worse than its bark.*

Why did the werewolf get a job as a comedian?
*Because he was a howl.*

Where do they send young werewolves who won't behave properly?
*To obedience school.*

# 11 Kooks & Spooks

What is the difference between a hungry monster and a greedy monster?
*One longs to eat, the other eats too long.*

What do you call a monster who's only 3 feet tall?
*"Shortie."*

What is a monster's normal eyesight?
*20-20-20-20.*

What do you get if you cross a giant and a skunk?
*A big stink.*

What do you get if you cross a vampire and a skunk?
*A dirty look from the vampire.*

What did King Kong say when his sister had a baby?
*"Well, I'll be a monkey's uncle!"*

Who delivers baby giants?
*Great big storks.*

What do ghosts do with their seatbelts when they get into an automobile?
*They boo-ckle (buckle) up.*

What kind of music do mummies like?
*Ragtime.*

What play by Shakespeare makes monsters cry?
*Romeo and Ghouliet.*

What do you get if you cross a mummy and a vampire?
*A gift-wrapped bat.*

Who goes to a zombie's party?
*Anyone who has an engraved invitation.*

Why did the vampire go sleepwalking in its pajamas?
*It didn't have a bat-robe.*

# Say These 3 Times Quickly

(TEE-HEE!)

The shiny sign says "Sharks."

The Blob bit a big black and brown bear and made the big black and brown bear bleed blood badly.

The shark ate the sheep and the cheap sheep soup.

The shark shook the shipshape ship sharply.

The Blob brought a black-backed bath brush.

The Blob's big blister bled.

PATIENT: Doctor, doctor! You've got to help me!
DOCTOR: Please calm down. Now, what seems to be the trouble?
PATIENT: I have this terrible feeling that I'm a werewolf.
DOCTOR: How long has this been going on?
PATIENT: Ever since I was a puppy.

What do werewolves call a fur coat?
*"Darling."*

How do you stop a man from changing into a werewolf in April?
*Shoot him in March.*

What do you get if you cross a werewolf and a witch?
*A mad dog that chases airplanes.*

IGOR: Did you hear about the man who died while doing a crossword puzzle?
BORIS: No, what happened?
IGOR: They buried him six down and three across.

Where do vampires plant flowers?
*In a bat-tanical (botanical) garden.*

Where do you buy an extinct animal?
*In a dino-store.*

What has 2 arms, 2 wings, 2 tails, 3 heads, 3 bodies and 8 legs?
*A man on a horse holding a chicken.*

VAMPIRE VICTIM: May I have a glass of water please?

VAMPIRE: Why, are you thirsty?

VAMPIRE VICTIM: No, I want to see if my neck leaks.

Why is Count Dracula so admired as a man of fashion?

*Because he's always dressed to kill.*

If you saw the Frankenstein monster standing on a handkerchief, how could you get the handkerchief without being in danger?

*Wait until he walked away.*

What is the difference between a ghost and a lame sailor?

*The ghost is a hobgoblin; the sailor is a gob hobblin'.*

What does a skeleton serve his dinner on?

*Bone china.*

How can you make a witch scratch?

*Take away its W.*

What do evil witches have for dessert at Chinese restaurants?

*Misfortune cookies.*

What wears a black cape, flies through the night, and bites people?

*A mosquito in a black cape.*

What happens if you cross a vampire and the most beautiful girl in the world?

*Nothing. Vampires won't allow themselves to be crossed.*

What did the Frankenstein monster say to the scarecrow?

*"I can beat the stuffing out of you."*

What do ghouls wear on their feet in the rain?

*Ghoul-oshes.*

Why did Count Dracula visit the orthodontist?
*For his bite.*

What disease does Count Dracula fear most?
*Tooth decay.*

Why does a vampire brush its teeth?
*To prevent bat-breath.*

What does a werewolf put on at the beach?
*Moon-tan lotion.*

# 12 Oh, No!

What happens to a pizza when it's 3,000 years old?
*It gets cold.*

Where do you leave messages for a ghoul?
*At the dead letter office.*

Five ghouls were sitting under an umbrella, but none of them got wet. How come?
*It wasn't raining.*

Why did the ghoul go to the beauty parlor?
*It heard that was the place people went to dye (die).*

What do you get if you cross King Kong and a parrot?

*A lot of big talk.*

What did the phantom say when it was guarding the cemetery?

*"Halt! Who ghost there?"*

What did the ghost say when its sheet ripped?

*"Well, I'll be darned!"*

What do you get if you cross a ghost with an alligator?

*An animal that says "Boo" before it bites.*

How does a skeleton study for a test?

*It bones up on it the night before.*

What does the Invisible Man call his mother and father?

*His transparents.*

How does a book about a zombie begin?

*With a dead-ication (dedication).*

"Now I'm taller than she is."
"Did you get a pair of elevator shoes?"
"No, she had her legs amputated."

What did the Frankenstein monster say when lightning struck him?

*Nothing. He was too shocked.*

What did the Frankenstein monster say when he ran out of electricity?
*"Oh, well, AC come, AC go."*

What did the boy Frankenstein monster say to the girl Frankenstein monster?
*"You are so electrocute."*

Where does a ghost keep his automobile?
*In a mirage (garage).*

Why are mummies always so selfish?
*Because they are all wrapped up in themselves.*

What does a giant do when he breaks his big toe?
*He calls a big toe (tow) truck.*

"Ma, why do I always walk in circles?"
"Keep quiet, kid, or I'll nail your other shoe to the floor."

Where does the Frankenstein monster go when he loses a hand?
*To a second-hand store.*

What would you get if you crossed an onion with a vampire?
*Either an onion that sucks blood or a vampire with watery eyes.*

Did you hear about the vampire who tried to bite a girl in the thick fog?
*He mist (missed).*

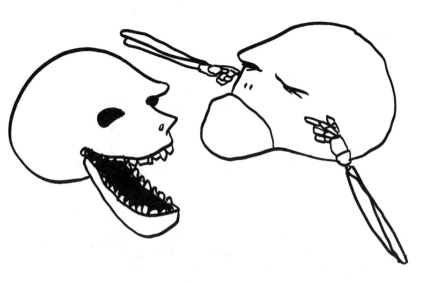

What do you call a skeleton that talks all the time?
*A jawbone.*

When do monsters know they are in love?
*When they love each shudder (other).*

Why did the monster nibble on the electric bulb?
*He only wanted a light snack.*

What does a polite vampire say to a lady at a dance?
*"May I have the necks vaults (next waltz)?"*

What is the only ailment that can stop a vampire?
*A stiff neck.*

Why can't you believe Count Dracula when he's resting in his coffin?
*Because he's lying.*

What do you call a cowardly sea serpent?
*Chicken of the Sea.*

What is the difference between a werewolf and a comma?
*A werewolf has claws at the end of its paws; a comma has a pause at the end of its clause.*

How does a werewolf file its claws?
*Under the letter "C."*

Why did the doctor order Count Dracula to take it easy?
*Because his blood pressure was too high.*

Mr. Monster woke at midnight in a terrible temper. "Where's my supper?" he yelled at his wife. "Where are my chains? Where is my poison? Where is my—"

"Now, hold on," Mrs. Monster said. "Can't you see I only have three hands?"

Why did the monster name both his sons Ed?
*Because two Eds (heads) are better than one.*

What happens when a vampire bites you?
*You get a drain (pain) in the neck.*

What always follows a werewolf?
*Its tail.*

What is the Frankenstein monster's favorite piece of furniture?
*An electric chair.*

Why are vampires most dangerous before dawn?
*Because they like to get a few bites before they go to sleep.*

Did you hear the story about the vampire's sharp teeth?
*Never mind, you wouldn't get the point.*

What kind of pictures does Count Dracula sketch?
*He likes to draw blood.*

Who was the most popular singer in prehistoric times?
*Dino Saur (Dinah Shore).*

# SAY THESE 3 TIMES QUICKLY
## (HEY-HEY!)

Frankenstein frees 55 frozen fleas.

The shark ate each sixth chick on the stick.

Most ghosts prefer preshrunk sheets.

The shark shocked seven short soldiers. Now, if the shark shocked seven short soldiers, where are the seven short soldiers the shark shocked?

Mrs. Smith's fish sauce shop.

How does one dinosaur tell another dinosaur to hurry up?

*"Pronto Saurus!"*

Is it true that mummies can keep a secret?

*Yes, they really know how to keep things under wraps.*

What happens if you don't pay your exorcist?

*You get repossessed.*

What happened when Count Dracula tried to write poetry?

*Things went from bat to verse.*

MONSTER BOY: Mummy! The lawn mower just cut off my foot!

MONSTER MOTHER: Well, stay outside until it stops bleeding. I just mopped the floor.

What did the giant say after he swallowed 16 sheep, 3 cows and 4 pigs?

*"Burp!"*

# 13 Zombies Can Be Fun

SAMMY: Dad, are there really ghosts?

FATHER: I don't know.

SAMMY: Are vampires bad?

FATHER: I don't know.

SAMMY: Do witches fly on broomsticks?

FATHER: I can't really say.

SAMMY: You don't mind my asking you all these questions, do you?

FATHER: Not at all. How are you going to learn anything if you don't ask questions?

Where did extinct animals go for the summer months?
*To the dino-shore.*

Where do ghosts go for sun and fun?
*To the sea ghost (coast).*

Did you hear the joke about the 50-foot giant?
*Never mind—it's way over your head.*

How do you help haunted eggs?
*Get an eggs-orcist (exorcist).*

Why don't ghosts like to go out in the rain?
*Because it dampens their spirits.*

Did you hear about the monster baby? He was so ugly, his parents sent him back and kept the stork.

What do you get if you cross a vampire with an Egyptian mummy?
*A flying Band-Aid.*

"How did you get that blow-out?"
"Ran over a pop bottle."
"Didn't you see it?"
"No. That kid had it under his arm."

Where does a ghost go for entertainment?
*To one of its favorite haunts.*

What instrument does a skeleton play?
*The trom-bone.*

What do dragons do to relax?
*They let off steam.*

Why didn't Count Dracula ever settle down?
*Because he was a fly-by-night.*

What is Count Dracula's favorite snack?
*Fangfurters.*

What is Count Dracula's favorite small building?
*A bloodshed.*

What kind of books do mummies read?
*Mysteries—they love to unravel them.*

FIRST ZOMBIE: Excuse me for living.
SECOND ZOMBIE: That's all right, but don't let it happen again.

What is the difference between zombies and darned socks?
*One is dead men, the other is men-ded.*

What is the hardest thing to sell a zombie?
*Life insurance.*

Who is safe from a man-eating shark?
*Women and children.*

The person who makes it does not need it.
The person who buys it does not use it.
The person who uses it does so without knowing.
What is it?
*A coffin.*

What do werewolves say on their Christmas cards?
*"Best vicious (wishes) of the season."*

Which roads do most vampires travel?
*The main arteries.*

Why do witches feel at home with turkeys?
*Because a turkey is always a-gobblin' (a goblin).*

When do monsters do well in school?
*When they use their heads.*

How do you make a skeleton laugh?
*Tickle its funny bone.*

How do you make a monster float?
*Take two scoops of ice cream, some root beer, one large monster . . .*

What is the difference between a monster and peanut butter?
*The monster doesn't stick to the roof of your mouth.*

What goes, "Ha, ha, ha, plop, plop, plop?"
*A monster laughing its heads off.*

If one Tyrannosaurus runs at 15 miles per hour, and another Tyrannosaurus runs at 25 miles per hour, what do you get if the two collide head-on?
*Tyrannosaurus Rex (wrecks).*

# SAY THESE 3 TIMES QUICKLY
## (UGH-UGH!)

Tyrannosaurus Rex wrecks wet rocks.

The Blob's black blank bank book.

Peggy Babcock's mummy.

The big bug's blood.

What do ghouls take when they have a sore throat?
*Coffin (coughin') drops.*

How do rattlesnakes talk to each other by telephone?
*Poison-to-poison.*

# 14 Sports Spectacular

FIRST VAMPIRE: I just met a fisherman who complained he hadn't had a bite all day.
SECOND VAMPIRE: So, what did you do?
FIRST VAMPIRE: What could I do? I bit him.

What does a vampire get when it bites a mummy?
*Practice.*

What is a vampire's favorite sport?
*Skin diving.*

What has 16 wheels and breathes fire?
*A dragon on roller skates.*

In what body of water do monsters like to swim?
*Lake Eerie (Erie).*

IGOR: If you had a gun with only one bullet and a monster was coming at you from one direction and a werewolf from the other, which would you shoot?

BORIS: I'd shoot the gun.

When do ghosts play baseball?
  *When their spirit is catching.*

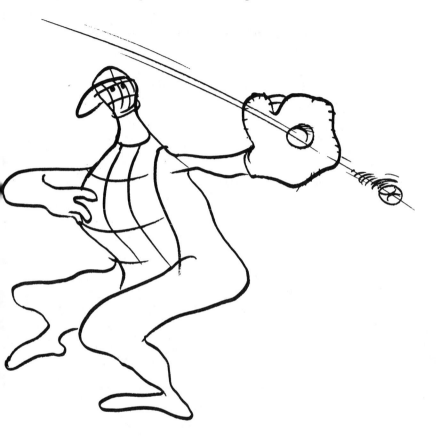

Where do dinosaurs race?
  *On dinosaur tracks.*

What kind of dinosaur can you ride in a rodeo?
  *A bronco-saurus.*

What kind of horses do zombies ride?
  *Nightmares.*

**What kind of car does Count Dracula own?**
*A bloodmobile.*

**What kind of car do most werewolves drive?**
*A wolfswagen.*

**What do you call a witch's motorcycle?**
*A ba-rooooom stick!*

**What did Count Dracula's son do on the baseball team?**
*He was the bat boy.*

**What kind of baseball game is popular with monsters?**
*A double-header.*

What is the monsters' favorite team?
*The Giants.*

Why was the mummy sent into the game as a pinch hitter?
*With a mummy at bat, the game would be all wrapped up.*

Why are so many funerals held in the library?
*Because many people like to have their noses buried in a book.*

What do they give to a shark who learns to dive to the bottom of the sea?
*A deep-loma (diploma).*

What is Count Dracula's favorite sport?
*Bat-minton (badminton).*

What is the difference between an Egyptian mummy and a crocodile?
*Well, if you don't know, you'd better not go swimming in the Nile.*

Where do zombies swim?
*In the Dead Sea.*

What is the best way to get rid of an evil spirit?
*Exorcise (exercise) a lot.*

Why are sharks poor tennis players?
*Because they don't like to get too close to the net.*

When is a shark dizzy?
*When its head is swimming.*

Why couldn't the Frankenstein monster play basketball?
*Because his sneakers were in the wash.*

What is worse than seeing a shark's fin in the water?

*Seeing its tonsils.*

Why are giants nice to have around?

*They're a ton of fun.*

# 15 Crazies

What is worse than a giraffe with a sore throat?
*A vampire with a toothache.*

What is green and only comes out at night?
*Vampickle.*

DRACULA: Knock, knock.
VICTIM: Who's there?
DRACULA: A-1.
VICTIM: A-1 what?
DRACULA: A-1 to drink your blood!

Why were the two vampires unable to marry?
*Because they loved in vein (vain).*

How can you tell if you have a giant in your bathtub?
*You can't close the shower curtain.*

What would you get if you crossed a bell and a large gorilla?
*You'd get a ding-dong King Kong.*

"Did you get the license number of the woman who ran over you?"
"No, but I'd recognize that laugh anywhere."

Which part of the house do ghosts like best?
*The die-ning (dining) room.*

Which branch of the service do werewolves join?
*The Hair Corps (Air Corps).*

Why was Dr. Jekyll upset?
*Things were getting under his Hyde (hide).*

IGOR: How do you lead a werewolf?
BORIS: It's simple. First you get a rope. Then you tie it to the werewolf—
IGOR: And then?
BORIS: And then you find out where he wants to go.

What kind of money do monsters use?
*Weirdo (weird dough).*

What is more frightening than a haunted house?
*Two haunted houses.*

Why does a mummy change when it is unwrapped?
*Because it is then a little bare (bear).*

Why are there so many vampires?
*Because a sucker is born every day.*

When was Count Dracula put in an insane asylum?
*When he went bats.*

FIRST MONSTER: My girlfriend has pedestrian eyes.
SECOND MONSTER: What are pedestrian eyes?
FIRST MONSTER: Eyes that look both ways before
they cross.

What would you get if you crossed a vampire with
a Volkswagen?
*A creature that attacks small cars and sucks
out their gas and oil.*

"Mom, when will we get a garbage can?"
"Shut up, kid, and keep eating."

What is the difference between a deer running from hunters and a short witch?

*One is a hunted stag; the other is a stunted hag.*

If you see a monster chasing four men, what time is it?

*One after four.*

What time is it when a monster sits on your watch?

*Time to get a new watch.*

What kind of candy won't a zombie ever touch?

*Life Savers.*

"Junior fell in the fireplace, Mom."
"Well, poke him up, son. It's chilly in here."

Which television game show do most sharks listen to?

*"Name That Tuna!"*

Where would you look for a lost dinosaur after a heavy rain?

*In a dino-sewer.*

What kind of mistake would it be if an undertaker buried a body in the wrong place?

*A grave mistake.*

What would you call a nervous witch?

*A twitch.*

On what kind of street does a zombie live?
*A dead-end street.*

What is a monster's favorite love song?
*"The Ghoul (Girl) That I Marry."*

What does a werewolf do when traffic is snarled?
*It snarls back.*

# 16 World Records

Who was the biggest monarch in history?
*King Kong.*

What is three stories tall, green, and laughs a lot?
*The Jolly Green Giant.*

A giant had three tongues. How did he remove two of them?
*He took off his shoes.*

Which is heavier—a half moon or a full moon?
*The full moon is lighter.*

What would you get if you crossed Godzilla with a kangaroo?

*Big holes all over Australia.*

Why did the dragon breathe on the map of the earth?

*Because he wanted to set the world on fire.*

Why did the dragon breathe fire on the village?

*Because he wanted to be the toast of the town.*

What is the hardest thing to do when a dragon breathes fire at you?

*Keep cool.*

"Other than that, Mrs. Lincoln, how did you like the play?"

What is big and hairy and flies 1,200 miles an hour?

*King Concorde.*

What was the first thing Count Dracula wanted to see when he visited New York City?

*The Vampire State Building.*

What kind of ghosts haunt skyscrapers?

*High spirits.*

What do they call the fattest female phantom?

*The ghostess with the mostess.*

Why is a skeleton like a lost sea treasure?

*Because it has a sunken chest.*

Which monster wears the biggest shoes?
*The one with the biggest feet.*

What is more invisible than an Invisible Man?
*His shadow.*

What would you get if you crossed the Loch Ness monster with a shark?
*Lockjaw.*

What would you get if you crossed a snail with Count Dracula?
*The world's slowest vampire.*

What country is haunted by ghosts?
*No country, only a terror-tory (territory).*

What famous monster discovered a new continent?
*Christopher Ghoulumbus (Columbus).*

What can you expect from a monster with 4 lips?
*Nothing but double talk.*

What would you get if you crossed a giant and a rooster?
*The biggest cluck in town.*

# 17 Things That Go Bump in the Night

What do you call a vampire that rides first class in an airplane?

*A passenger.*

FIRST HUNTER: Did I tell you about the time I met a giant in the woods?

SECOND HUNTER: No, you didn't. Did you give him both barrels?

FIRST HUNTER: Both barrels? I gave him the whole gun!

**115**

When did the mad scientist stop being lonely?
*When he learned how to make friends.*

How did the Frankenstein monster feel about lightning?
*It gave him a big charge.*

How do you fit five giants in a Volkswagen?
*Two in the front, two in the back, and one in the glove compartment.*

When a monster travels on an airplane, where does he sit?
*Anywhere he wants to.*

What goes "Thump, thump, thump, swish, thump, thump, thump, swish?"
*A monster with a wet sneaker.*

What weighs 2,000 pounds and is all bone?
*A skele-ton.*

What slows a vampire down?
*Tired blood.*

MOTHER MONSTER: Don't you think Junior has a mechanical mind?
FATHER MONSTER: He certainly does. I wish he wouldn't forget to wind it up every morning.

Would you rather have a werewolf attack you—or a vampire?
*I'd rather have them attack each other.*

How did Jack defeat the giant?
*He used his bean.*

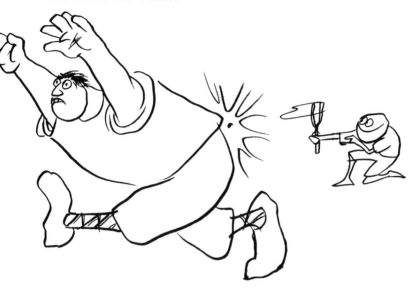

What do you get if you cross a giant with a vampire?
*A BIG pain in the neck.*

What do you get if you cross a vampire with a hyena?
*An animal that laughs at the sight of blood.*

What do you get if you cross a vampire with a ghoul?
*I don't know. No one has ever wanted to hang around long enough to find out.*

Why didn't the genie like being in the bottle?
*Because it was a jarring experience.*

When does a graveyard romance start?
*When boy meets ghoul.*

Why do demons and ghouls get along so well together?
*Because demons (diamonds) are a ghoul's (girl's) best friend.*

Why did the knight attack an insect?
*Because it was a dragonfly.*

Why do dragons sleep during the day?
*So they can fight knights (nights).*

Where did knights learn to kill dragons?
*In knight school.*

What ghost haunts an educational building?
*The school spirit.*

What happens to a mummy when it falls into the Nile?
*It gets wet.*

What is the difference between a kangaroo and a mummy?
*One bounds around; the other is bound around.*

Why did they have to put a fence around the cemetery?
*Because people were dying to get in.*

FATHER ZOMBIE: Please don't sit in that chair, son.
SON ZOMBIE: Why not, Dad?
FATHER ZOMBIE: We're saving that for Rigor Mortis to set in.

Why did the skeleton use toothpaste?
*To keep its teeth from falling out.*

Why didn't the skeleton go to school?
*Because his heart wasn't in it.*

How do you make any skeleton fat?
*Throw him up in the air and he will come down "plump!"*

Where can a monster always find sympathy?
*In the dictionary.*

What do you get if you cross a vampire with a snowball?

*Frostbite.*

What do you get if you cross a jolly, fat man in a red suit with a werewolf?

*Santa Claws.*

SANTA

What do you get if you cross a cocker spaniel, a poodle, and a ghost?

*A cock-a-poodle-boo!*

Two young children stood in front of a mummy case in the museum. On the bottom of the mummy case they noticed "1286 B.C."

"What does the number mean?" asked the first one.

The second one thought and said, "That must be the license of the car that hit him."

How do you get a giant out of a box of Cracker Jacks?

*Read the directions on the back of the box.*

How can you tell that a giant is under your bed?

*Your nose touches the ceiling.*

What happened when Count Dracula met the pretty girl?

*It was love at first bite.*

**121**

What do you get if you cross a rooster and a werewolf?

*An animal that howls when the sun comes up.*

What do you get if you cross a werewolf and a zebra?

*A killer in a striped suit.*

What kind of fur do you get from a werewolf?

*As fur as you can get.*

What do you get if you cross a pet dog and a werewolf?

*A new owner every full moon.*

Why shouldn't you pull a dinosaur by the tail?

*It may only be his tail, but it could be your*